GRIEFWORK
IS ESSENTIAL
NOT OPTIONAL

Let the healing continue…

A Memoir of Overcoming
Grief,
Depression,
& Rejection

Dr. Tonya Cunningham

Published by Dr. Tonya Cunningham.
www.drtonyacunningham.com

ISBN: 978-0-578-80946-5

This book is dedicated to
Every person who has experienced loss of any kind
Families hit by the coronavirus outbreak (COVID-19)
Mankind experiencing global crisis (mass loss)
Those who struggle to embrace new normalcy
Essential Workers in the trenches

Table of Contents

Foreword

By Carla R. Cannon
"The Trailblazer"

I have had the honor of serving as Tonya's Life Coach and mentor since 2016, and what an honor it has been to watch her grow and evolve into the woman, teacher, ministry leader and entrepreneur she is today! Coaching Tonya has been a complete honor because although she is called to lead others, she also knows how to be led. Although I am younger than Tonya, she has trusted my wisdom and guidance, and I am truly humbled to be included in this amazing body of work.

Tonya's heart is so tender toward hurting people who are desperately seeking inner healing. Within her first book, I Got My Marbles Back, Tonya provided you with a sneak peek into her life by sharing some of her most intimate moments of self-discovery, inner healing and a path that led her to where she is today. Upon meeting her, I could see the prophetic mantle that is upon her life, and I know one day soon, I will witness her walk into it. Coining her as "The Grief Doctor" was me simply sharing with her what I heard the Lord say. I believe this was before she received her doctorate. However, Tonya's skill is beyond her multiple degrees, for she has endured the pain of loss and now teaches others how to do the same while creating new memories as they walk through their healing journey.

A doctor is defined as someone who is skilled to treat sick and injured people. This describes Tonya perfectly. Her calling is to breathe life back into individuals who have experienced trauma and feel as though they are beyond recovery. Tonya's favorite phrase holds to be true, "There IS life after loss; it's just a different one!"

Within this new body of work, *Griefwork is Essential, Not Optional*, Tonya takes you on a deeper journey into her life as she unveils her fears, traumas and past mistakes all in an effort to lead her readers into greater healing as well. Knowing Tonya personally and professionally has allowed me to see different parts of her which are all consistent with her life's work. She is a woman who loves God deeply and has endured a great level of pain for the mantle that currently rests upon her life. Tonya is more than qualified to teach you how to press through as you learn how to breathe again after enduring some of life's greatest punches.

Through her passion of helping others heal, Tonya understands that her personal journey of inner healing must continue as well, and she does so unapologetically and gracefully. Tonya is what some would call a "preacher's preacher" or a "leader's leader" because her heart is truly toward those who have a great calling on their life and often suffer in silence. Tonya not only offers her shoulder but her couch as well through Grief Coaching. Her transparent approach makes her relatable, her passion causes you to feel connected to her, and her experience causes you to trust her because she is not leading you down a path she has not had to walk.

In the midst of it all, Tonya is still standing today after experiencing the loss of both of her parents, a child, her marriage and various friendships along the way. There is no pain that the Grief Doctor cannot relate to. Therefore, I encourage you to take a moment to pause and pray before you journey any further within the pages of this book because it may hurt first before you experience healing. But I promise if you stay the course, the pain you feel will be mended as you continue to do your soul work.

Tonya, thank you for your continual love, support and respect. I truly admire you, and because of you, I too have committed to a lifetime of healing. I am experiencing self-awareness in a way I never thought was possible prior to meeting you. You are truly a world changer! As I prophesied to you in 2018 at the Emerge Conference, God is going to take you all around the WORLD! Get ready! Hopefully Texas has appreciated you, because you will not be as available real soon! Mark my words; for it shall happen!

Carla R. Cannon
"The Trailblazer"
Business & Lifestyle Strategist & Author
www.CarlaCannon.com

A Note to Readers

This book was designed to serve as a resource for those experiencing emotional pain of any kind due to life transitions. The ultimate goal for you, as the reader, is to identify areas of loss and their impact on your life.

As you journey through the pages of this literary work, seek to find your life story within the memoir of my life story. While doing so, please seek professional intervention if you feel overwhelmed during your reading process.

Understand that there is healing value nestled down within your story and that secrets can heal once they are exposed to light. Overcoming emotional trauma gets to the root of healing because our deepest wounds lurk in our psyche.

This book offers options for you to unveil, excavate, and heal your hidden hurt. It is the sequel to my best-selling book *I Got My Marbles Back: There IS Life After Loss.* If you haven't done so already, I encourage you to read *I Got My Marbles Back* to understand the groundwork of *Griefwork is Essential Not Optional.*

TELL YOUR STORY

"Through stories, we discover the truth of our human experience: just think of the many stories and movies you love because they reinforce your values or your sense of humor, or hold an important message. Many of our oldest stories — fables, fairytales, and parables — hold within them a moral message, expressed through archetypal characters and, often, magical messengers. Like Little Red Riding Hood should not have left the path in the woods to encounter the talking wolf; Beauty needed to love the handsome prince even when he looked like a beast. There are tales of entrapment and escape in Rapunzel, Hansel and Gretel, and Bluebeard, the jealousy of the ugly sisters in Cinderella, and the Little Match Girl's extreme poverty. Reading today's memoirs, we find the same themes: challenge, courage, transformation, and reward. In telling your story, you write only what you, uniquely, know while reaching out to others who have shared your experiences."

Reasons to Write Your Memoir

To write out difficult emotions, such as guilt, anger, or loss

To share extraordinary and ordinary events that have meaning for you

To make sense of the past

To record your family history

To celebrate a family event

Because you want to [1]

My Creative Life: Rediscover Your Creativity by Liz Dean

---

[1] (Dean 2019)

Life Happens...

"We cannot tell what may happen to us in the strange medley of life. But we can decide what happens IN us… and that is what really counts in the end. How to take the raw stuff of life and make it a thing of worth and beauty."

Joseph Fort Newton

Introduction:
Let the Healing Continue...

The still popular fairytale story of Cinderella continues to influence the world today. Its relevance grabs the attention of the viewer because of the relatable subjects shared in the storyline. It's often referred to as a modern day 'Rags to Riches' story about a young girl who went from a life of oppression and unrecognition to triumph and reward. Generally, the plot of most fairytale stories finishes with a happy ending. Cinderella marries Prince Charming in an elegant storybook wedding, and they live happily ever after. So we are told.

MY STORY

From the moment my elementary school teacher read this epic story to our class, I secretly dreamed of one day marrying my Prince Charming and riding off into the sunset with him. Yes. This little black girl born in the mid-1960s, during the most turbulent decade in history at that time, was able to escape reality through dreaming. Despite the tumultuous experience of the Civil Rights Movement that was at an all-time high, as a six-year-old, I frequently envisioned leaving the community in which I lived to marry my Prince Charming. I dreamt he would search for me, find me, sweep me off my feet, and carry me off to a better life. Little did I know I would spend the majority of my life awaiting his arrival.

Even though faced with pressure from society to get married, because my internal clock was ticking, I'd like to think I didn't buckle under the intimidation from others to jump into marriage just to experience the wedding day, complete with a beautiful white gown. I wholeheartedly and intentionally waited for the one I believed God chose for me. With confidence, I combatted the questions. "Why are you still single? You don't want to be an old maid getting married, do you?" I remained in readiness, preparing for the purposes of marriage by becoming a confident, self-sufficient, single woman. I held on to Proverbs 18:22, believing the right man would find me.

Finally, the day came when I met my Prince Charming. Interestingly enough, I didn't see him as such at that time. We met at church, and for several years, we were friends and served well alongside each other in a local church. Out of nowhere, something changed within me. I secretly started liking him. No one knew I liked him except God. I wouldn't dare express my feelings because he was not the man I dreamed about marrying, and neither was I the young bride, waiting for him. The Prince

Charming I created in my head was six feet tall, slim with smooth chocolate skin and coal-black wavy hair.

One day, he asked me out on a date. I accepted without hesitation because of my attraction to him, which I now perceive was the anointing of God upon his life. I've since learned that the anointing on someone is very attractive. Thus, this is the reason so many ministry leaders in the church succumb to weakness and sin—they can't handle the attraction the anointing brings.

We had only one date. Midway through it, he proposed.

He pulled out a little black box and asked, "Will you be my queen for the Kingdom of God?"

In shock, my heart stood still for a moment which seemed like eternity. "Yes," I screamed and then leaped out of the car into his arms.

We double dated with another couple (our friends) that was present to witness this monumental occasion of two spiritual powerhouses coming together as one. Later, during the date-now engagement, I learned they knew about the proposal. He went to them and our spiritual father for advice about proposing to me. He felt led by God to marry me. And interestingly enough, I felt led by God to marry him, a man a decade younger than I was. We both professed that what we felt was the leading of the Holy Spirit, so we got engaged and then started dating. The exact opposite of what society dictates for marriage, the road we chose together, our fairytale. Or shall I say MY fairytale?

Our wedding was a picturesque event, filled with the gamut of emotions a wedding day can bring. Hundreds of people filled the majestic sanctuary of the church to capacity, there to witness our nuptials and either share in our joy or simply spectate. The long aisle stretched down the middle of the room. Fresh, cut flowers released a gentle scent, and stain-glassed windows filtered sunlight through the windows as the sun set. The moment I awaited all my life finally arrived — time for me to walk down the aisle into the arms of my Prince Charming.

The doors slowly opened, giving me one last opportunity to gaze into the eyes of my father, thinking, "I'm about to marry a man like you, Daddy, who will love me and protect me like you have since childhood." I smiled and took the first step down the aisle as the hand-bell choir played the traditional bridal march. So majestic! "Here Comes the Bride" resounded through the massive sanctuary, filling me with great anticipation of a life with my Prince Charming.

A writer, Brela Delahoussaye, states in one of her writings, "A great marriage requires choosing to stay in love through the high of the highs and the low of the lows…every day."

As two imperfect individuals, uninformed about marriage, we did not traverse the rocky terrain of our marriage well. There were several situations that contributed to its demise.

First of all, we had only one pre-marital counseling session. It was a huge mistake that we didn't seek out further pre-marital counsel. Let's not forget, we didn't date. We were engaged and married nine months later.

Our attempt to date between engagement and marriage was overshadowed by the demands of planning a wedding.

We also faced tragedy three days prior to the wedding when our wedding coordinator, my mentor, was brutally murdered. From the moment we said, "I do," our lives drastically changed. Married in June 2003, we started a church in September 2003. Two new babies (our marriage and church) were born less than 90 days apart. The very next year, our baby girl, Chelsea, was born prematurely without warning and died hours later. Soon after that, we took a troubled boy from the church into our home, then my mother died, and later on we adopted another teenage boy.

These were only a few of the monumental obstacles we faced as a young, ill-prepared couple. All together, these ingredients were a recipe for a failed marriage. Not to mention the unaddressed brokenness within each of us. Without the proper tools and foundation, our marriage was destined to fail. It was only a matter of time.

I've since learned that marriage can be wonderful. However, it requires work and commitment from both parties. It takes two people to build a relationship, but only one to destroy it. After a while, it appeared that the light of joy within my husband had dimmed. I later learned it was snuffed out by his inability to continue in a marriage he did not want, forcing him to hide his true feelings. Looking back, I can vividly see the dysfunction in our marriage. The sad indictment is I didn't realize it until we were headed to divorce court, and even then, I did not see the totality of it all. My life story began to unfold for deeper healing.

After nine years of marriage, the bottom of my world fell out from underneath me as my husband (and pastor) announced his desire to move on in life without me.

He stated, "I no longer have the capacity to be married to you any longer."

To this day, that statement is etched into the fabric of my psyche. I thought to myself, "What does THAT mean?" I kept awaiting an explanation of what he meant, BUT it never came. His statement left me feeling broken and worthless.

Later, after our separation and divorce, it was revealed to me that he released himself from our marriage to be fully present in the LGBTQ Community.

After hearing of our separation, a gay guy brought me a book and said, "Here, read this. It'll help you understand what just happened to you so you won't go down this road again."

I attempted to read the book entitled, *On the Down Low* by J. L. King but got no further than the book dedication which reads, "I dedicate this book to all the women whose health has been jeopardized and emotional state compromised by men living on the DL, and to all women in general who may use this book as a protective guide. I also dedicate this book to men on the DL in hopes that looking in this mirror will be a catalyst to change."

The news of this murdered my soul, leaving me grief stricken, suicidal. I closed the book cover and didn't read it until later on in my healing journey.

While my flesh wanted to be revengeful, the Spirit of God wouldn't allow me to. Throughout the divorce proceedings, I struggled with grief, depression, anxiety, abandonment, and rejection just to name a few. There was a constant war going on within me. I kept hearing the promise of God reverberate in my spirit, "I am with you." However, my flesh continued a rebuttal toward the Spirit of God with doubt and questions. "Was my marriage real? Is God really real?"

In desperation, I admitted myself to a mental health hospital because life had stripped me of everything: love, marriage, family, church, friends, and identity. It was in that locked unit that my healing began. I submitted to the process of healing so my faith and feelings could stop colliding, releasing me from the perpetual internal emotional war.

Let's fast forward. It's 2020, the unprecedented, yet monumental year that changed the world due to the global pandemic—COVID-19. Eight years post-separation/divorce, and I'm thriving emotionally, physically, spiritually, and financially but not without a cost. The crown of thriving comes with the cross of doing the work to heal.

Bishop T.D. Jakes said, "Every crown is paid for by a cross."

It has been a long, hard journey of working through the grief, depression, rejection, abandonment, betrayal, anger and forgiveness.

Of this long list of issues, depression, anger, rejection, and forgiveness were the hardest to navigate through. I was a middle-aged churchless and vulnerable divorcee who had to be willing to participate in my own healing by doing my griefwork. In doing so, I've learned that one of the greatest causes of emotional trauma is divorce and abandonment.

Deliverance and inner healing expert, Dr. Henry Malone, says, "There is no such thing as an amiable divorce."

This is so true because we don't enter marriage thinking it will fail. Our hope is to stay together until death parts us. The hard reality is everyone connected to the marriage gets hurt. From the couple, children, grandchildren, parents, grandparents, siblings, aunts, uncles, cousins, friends, to colleagues. The entire family unit is impacted!

I lived a sheltered life and was naïve about life. While I honestly did not know about my former husband's internal struggle with his sexuality and identity, I did know our marriage was rocky from day one and that something was off. Looking back, I can see the big, red neon flags that were present. My countless attempts to connect with him during our marriage were unsuccessful. Creating moments to converse with him about what was bothering him failed. Sadly, he didn't trust me with him. It hurt to know that we went from being close friends who talked often to married roommates who communicated primarily through email. One of the regrets I have is that I was not a safe place for him to land.

Always remember that healing is a journey and not a destination. It's a lifelong process that involves the investment of your time and emotions to cultivate a healthy lifestyle. Through personal work of my own, counseling, talking with my village of supporters/spiritual advisors, and coaching with Coach Carla R. Cannon, I've learned *not* to be a professional red flag collector. I no longer see the red flags of dysfunction and then choose to do nothing about them. Having grown and healed in certain areas of my life, here are just a *few* of the red flags I identified.

RED FLAGS AND LESSONS LEARNED

- **Red Flag**—thrusted my childhood image and desire of Prince Charming on him.

Lesson—heal from childhood trauma, which will enable you to deal with your reality.

- **Red Flag**—focused only on a fairytale wedding rather than the relationship.

Lesson—marriage is not about a wedding day, but a healthy life together.

- **Red Flag**—his proposal question of, "Will you be my queen for the Kingdom of God?"

Lesson—be fully present in the relationship so that you can discern what is *really* being communicated.

This was a request to help him build a church, not to marry him and spend our lives together. He was of the COGIC (Church of God in Christ) denomination foundationally, which leaned heavily on the public image of a pastor and his wife (the First Lady), an idealistic, non-scriptural title fabricated by the black church. I could write a book about this topic alone.

- **Red Flag**—we spiritualized everything and did not deal with the practical or emotional issues present.

As human beings, we are comprised of spirit, body, and soul. To live a holistic healthy life, each dimension of who we are must be cultivated and nurtured.

Lesson—there is a spiritual, emotional and practical approach to healing; each area must be dealt with.

Do not over spiritualize things to where you neglect the practicality of what's really happening.

Healing can feel like undergoing surgery without anesthesia. It's a tearing and ripping of your emotional flesh to get to the infected, wounded area that's limiting your life expectancy. Oftentimes, the healing and recovery phase hurts more than the surgery.

It was very difficult to navigate through the grief, depression, rejection, etc. due to unresolved preexisting issues from my lineage that I was unaware of. This discovery was unveiled and revealed to me as I went on the healing journey. This is why it is so important that each of us take personal responsibility in healing from both past and current issues because unresolved hurt, pain, or grief, do not go away. It remains dormant, awaiting its debut during the next crisis in your life.

Divorce was the tool that provoked me to heal. I believe nothing is wasted—the good and the bad are working together for good in our lives. I am forever indebted to my former husband for our transitional marriage because I cannot talk about my healing journey without talking about our marriage and divorce. It was the catalyst that opened the reservoir of past emotional trauma in my life. It identified the layers of unresolved issues in my life that still needed to be shed.

Part I
Overcoming Grief

Time does not change us. It just unfolds us.

Max Frisch

Chapter 1
Spill the Beans

In my grief counseling practice, I have found that many clients avoid counseling because they perceive it as a "spilling the beans" session, a time of divulging secrets. When beans spill, they roll all over the place, leaving the person who spilled them with the task of cleaning up a mess. This analogy is applicable to real life. When secrets are shared, emotions explode and spill all over the place, leaving you feeling helpless and out of control.

The sad indictment upon this belief is that the secret could possibly be a parasite to their pain, draining them, rendering them lifeless. Nonetheless, most choose not to participate in any form of counseling. Meanwhile, back at the ranch, their lives are falling apart—privately and publicly. Because what we hide soon oozes out for public consumption.

Therefore, it is true that sharing *is* the bedrock of counseling. However, counseling is also a collaborative work between the counselor and the counselee. The only way to receive the benefits of it is for the counselee to participate in their own rescue. Which means truth *must* be shared with the counselor. I too was guilty of holding secrets until the tragedy of a painful and public divorce came along and shattered my world in 2012. The years 2012 through 2020 have been transitional years for me. The ending of my old identity and the beginning of the new, true, authentic, God-ordained identity. Transformation and change has to begin internally.

The late Dr. Myles Munroe once said, "When a person has to be told to change, you are wasting your time. Information doesn't bring transformation, conversion does." Pastor Ray Taylor, my pastor, preached a message on February 17, 2019 entitled, "Let Us Go On" encouraging us to move from where we are to where God is calling us. Here's an excerpt from that message which resonates with me to this day.

"Diligence is not a natural trait because we naturally seek comfort. Diligence requires development and consistency. You can be taught a skill and strategy, but not effort. Be diligent and go through every step. Progress has a price tag called process. Avoid the pain of the process, you avoid progress. Change requires loss and causes conflict. Conflict causes pain."

I acknowledge that I was a former information junky — always gathering data but never executing. Learning to endure the pain of the process has helped me grow because I cannot conquer what I'm unwilling to confront.

My pivotal "spill the beans" moment occurred in outpatient therapy in 2012. This was immediately after spending six days and six nights in a mental health hospital. I met an earth angel affectionately known as "Grandpa."

Here's an excerpt about him from my book, *I Got My Marbles Back: There IS life after loss.*

An older Caucasian gentleman, a chaplain, approached me after my first day in group. He said, "Pastor Tonya, I don't know who you are, but God told me to tell you, He's gonna make you spill the beans. Now I don't know what that means, but I believe that you know what I'm referring to. Rest assured that God sees and knows what's going on. [2]

This man whom I never met before continued to exhort and share the word of the Lord with me. He said, "You are God's Girl. He's trying you in the fire, but you will come out as pure gold. The root of bitterness is gonna try and set in on ya. Identify it and put it under the blood of Jesus. God has a plan for your life."

Divorce is devastating! It's the death of a dream, and the pain of it cuts deep. It is worse than others realize, affecting not only the couple but everyone attached to them. As I shuffled through all the hurt and pain of our divorce, my counselor helped me *spill the beans* concerning my marriage. She helped me identify all the beans (secrets) and collateral damage associated with the marriage and subsequent divorce such as:

- Prior to his death, my mentor, Dr. Gregory W. Spencer, asked me if I was sure about marrying my now former husband. At the time, I didn't understand his question. While going through the healing process, I later discerned the message behind his question.
- Guilt over not dating nor getting pre-marital counseling.

[2] (Cunningham 2015)

16

- Guilt from not addressing the pain inflicted upon others over starting a church 90 days after getting married.

- The aftermath of tension caused by my husband asking me to marry him again in a private setting. I didn't understand his need to ask again, but instead of asking, I allowed the action to create doubt in me.

- Hurt over taking a troubled young teenage boy into our home immediately after the death of our baby.

- Shame and guilt over my naivety of red flags prior to and during the marriage, trying to understand the issues and work to resolve them. As a newlywed, I didn't share these concerns with anyone, denying that my dream future might be in jeopardy. I ignored some problems:

  ➢ Marriage not consummated until three days after the wedding
  ➢ Constant conflict between us
  ➢ Lack of intimacy in the marriage
  ➢ Avoidance
  ➢ His late night outings

- Denial of prophetic dreams God downloaded during and post marriage.

- Guilt over marrying a man 11 years younger. We were both powerful but in different leagues.

- Angry for seven years of living in fear due to yearly HIV/AIDS testing mandated by my PCP.

- Anger regarding countless people who approached me after the divorce about his struggle with sexual identity. As his wife, why didn't I see his struggles?

• Guilt over feelings of still desiring to protect him when he has been seen several times in gay clubs, living his life while I was struggling emotionally. Even in writing this book, I don't want to make him the "bad guy." Part of me still wants to protect him, although I share the truth of my emotions to heal and help others find healing too.

• Anger when I encounter many women who live in this situation, never suspecting the hidden truths of their husbands' secret lives. This is true not only for those involved in LGBTQ but also in any infidelity, addictions or other destructive habits. And in many cases, when the truth surfaces, the unsuspecting spouse struggles with far more than the broken dream. I am not comforted by knowledge of the unwanted sisterhood, women in similar situation of hidden truths.

My counselor helped me unveil and excavate all the hidden hurt, collateral damage, and so much more in the marriage. A major takeaway from my counseling experience is that strength is found in your vulnerability. Once you find a safe place to spill the beans, you'll begin to see healing unfold for you. As a direct result of that excavation process, it tilled the ground of my heart, preparing me to unveil, excavate, and heal from pre-existing hurt that had nothing to do with him.

As I mentioned previously, healing is hard work. I endeavored to get in the trenches and do the work to maintain my healing from the divorce, but I always felt a push back. It was like a dark cloud hovering over me at all times. In June

2016, I purchased a book about inner healing and deliverance entitled *Shadow Boxing* by Dr. Henry Malone. The spirit of procrastination and life busyness had a tight grip on me, so I didn't read it until April 2020. The pressure of the pandemic forced me to read the book, and I am so happy I read it because it changed my life! In a worldwide pandemic (COVID-19), this book kicked my healing journey into overdrive. Information from this book helped me realize I wasn't crazy for feeling as if a glass ceiling tottered over my head. Despite genuine efforts to heal, I couldn't push past issues in my life. It gave insight and explained the necessity of healing from my past emotional trauma of depression, rejection, anxiety, pride, and abandonment. Since then, I've gone through personal inner healing sessions with my Inner Healing Mentor as well as participated in trainings for inner healing and deliverance.

Now, I am able to embrace the collateral beauty found after tragedies. I can appreciate the time lived with my former husband. He's a brilliant guy, and I learned so much from him. In truth, we were two broken people who attempted to live a whole life together without addressing our past pain. I believe we both loved each other, but unfortunately, it was not the kind of love and commitment needed for marriage.

I am now a thriving adult in continual pursuit of health and wealth in all areas of my life. I teach others to thrive through trauma, pain, and loss and to understand that thriving is a learned behavior that will catapult them beyond just surviving.

Pivotal Moment: an important point that signifies a shift in direction

How you handle your pivot is going to impact your outcome.

The divorce was my pivotal moment to awaken me to the need for healing.

Identify the *beans* (secrets) that are holding you hostage and impeding your healing.

_____

_____

_____

_____

_____

_____

_____

_____

_____

_____

_____

_____

Recovery Toolkit: excavation and irrigation tools

Choose to heal and allow yourself to spill the beans. Commit to finding your safe space to share, be it with a counselor, spiritual advisor, or mentor, through journaling, or simply talking with family or friends.

List the ways that you are doing or plan to do the work of healing through sharing.

_____

_____

_____

_____

_____

_____

_____

_____

_____

_____

_____

_____

I cannot change the hurt of my past, but I can decide to stand tall in my healing and march forward with my lessons in hand and heart intact.

Alex Elle

Chapter 2
Are You Ready to Change?

In his book, *Leadership Pain: The Classroom for Growth*, leadership expert Samuel R. Chand states, "Growth equals change; change equals loss; loss equals pain; so inevitably, growth equals pain."

In reality, everything is always changing and evolving, no matter how hard we try to keep things the same. The hardcore truth is that anything not changing is not growing. In the world of 'grief,' *change* and *adjustment* are two major components in the healing process because grief changes who you are.

Grief is the natural, normal reaction to any significant loss, whether it's a death loss or a non-death loss. The negative impact of grief on individuals, families, businesses, and organizations is universal because grief is not about death only. It is about loss. Grief crosses all cultures and socioeconomic backgrounds, leaving the griever struggling to find their *new normal*.

After a significant loss, it is important to understand that nothing's the same. One of the biggest mistakes made after a loss is an attempt to go back to life like it was prior to the loss.

The death of a loved one can be devastating, turning your whole world upside down and out of balance. The person you were prior to the death drifted out to sea and will never return; therefore, in order to heal, it's important to stop expecting your *old self* to surface or come back to shore. Why is it important to do this? The answer is because everything in your life has changed, especially you. Your belief system, routines such as sleeping and eating, emotional stability, relationships and even your perception in life have taken on a different meaning. Your comfort zone no longer exists. Therefore, a new identity needs to be created.

You may say, "But I don't want a new identity. I was fine just the way I was!"

Accepting the reality of a new situation does not mean you cut off the past and deny the existence of your loved one or what you lost. It simply means you build on that past to create a *new you*.

Despite how we may dislike it, we are different than before the loss. Our lives are *totally* different. Without our permission, grief changed us. *Normal* seems like something hanging in outer space — light years away. Unfortunately, this uncomfortable abode becomes the new normal.

Often, bereaved people find that their grief can be misunderstood by others who have not experienced the same kind of loss, who have not yet faced the death of someone they love deeply or who was an integral part of their lives. Sometimes in grief, it can seem nearly impossible to understand yourself, much less find others who can understand.

Adjusting to find your *new norm* is not like surfing the web to find a new home, a new vacation spot, a new doctor, or mechanic. When searching for something *new* in our society, happy emotions are generally associated with that search. However, finding our *new normal* after a loss is painful and takes months and oftentimes years of hard work. Grief never ends—it modifies and softens. Embracing your *new normal* requires acceptance that things will never go back to the way it was prior to the loss.

You must ask yourself a question, because if nothing changes, nothing changes. "Am I ready to transform from my destructive habits?"

While this may sound easy to accomplish, trust me, it is not. As human beings, we develop behaviors, be it productive or destructive. From birth, we morph into creatures of habit. We like what we like, *how* we like it, *when* and *where* we like it. When the need arises to alter our destructive habits, we avoid change because it is hard work! If modifications were easy, then our world would be a better place to live.

We can repeatedly declare the Nike shoe company slogan, 'Just Do It,' but that doesn't bring about transformation. Change must first take place in the mind, the control tower for your body. Whatsoever a man thinks, so is he. The challenge comes because grief causes emotional injury. If not addressed, it sometimes produces lasting damage psychologically and emotionally, therefore, leaving you brokenhearted, trying to make adjustments for your betterment. For most, it is an impossible feat to do so alone. This is why counseling is so vital, because it allows you to get help in areas where you are paralyzed due to grief—this tangled ball of emotions such as denial, depression, abandonment, sorrow, confusion, anxiety, sadness, rage, bitterness, rejection, helplessness, loneliness, betrayal, fear, inadequacy, resentment, anguish, hurt, and the list goes on.

The process of change is difficult to tread because it involves the death of familiarity. We must be willing to pass through spaces of unfamiliarity and discomfort to get to our place of healing.

One must push past the obstacles of transformation and learn to create a new normal from trauma's aftermath. Learning to create a sense of balance and embrace a holistic approach to grief is essential to the griever. Balance aids in the healing process and maintains stability in all arenas of your life—emotional, spiritual, psychological and physical.

Before we can hope to shift and do our griefwork, we must be ready to face our fear of the unknown, our shame of hiding the truth from the world and ourselves, our denial of the need to change, and our pride blocking our ability to reach out for the help we need to adjust.

Sadly, the lack of change in my marriage led to its demise. Marriage works, if you work it.

You can rediscover life after tragedy if you embrace and apply alteration to your life.

So again, I ask, are you ready to change? Many say they are ready, but they are not willing to do whatever it takes to make change happen.

Pivotal Moment: an important point that signifies a shift in direction

How you handle your pivot is going to impact your outcome.

My mental breakdown was the pivotal moment that provoked me to change.

Identify your pivotal moment(s) that unveiled your need for change.

_____

_____

_____

_____

_____

_____

_____

_____

_____

_____

_____

Recovery Toolkit: excavation and irrigation tools

Assess if you are really ready to make the necessary adjustments for change to take place in your life. Journal your thoughts.

_____

_____

_____

_____

_____

_____

_____

_____

_____

_____

_____

_____

_____

_____

Every human being carries grief, if only for the little, everyday losses. Grief is a process with a host of emotions.

Life After Loss: Conquering Grief and Finding Hope
Raymond Moody, Jr, MD & Dianne Arcangel

Chapter 3
The Work of Grief

AFTER THE BREAK

In August 2019, at age 53, I traveled abroad for the very first time. Since the death of my marriage, traveling was one of the new things I desired to do. So needless to say, this trip represented much more than mere travel. It spoke of newness of life and freedom.

My travel buddy and friend since middle school traveled with me. We visited Rome, Italy, Florence, Italy, and Paris, France. During a joyous trip, we created memories for a lifetime. However, on day four of the eight-day vacation, I ran into a bump in the road. Literally.

While running across the uneven cobblestone pavement in Florence, Italy, I fell and injured my hand and leg. Although I had never experienced a broken bone before, I knew my hand was broken but feared seeking medical attention in a foreign country. So I hopped to the nearest pharmacy and purchased a gauze wrap to immobilize my wrist. Once my friend wrapped my wrist, we continued on our adventure. This experience taught me the power of the mind. Because I invested time and money into this trip, I mentally willed myself to keep pushing forward through the pain caused by the break — to the point the aching was not a major issue.

Yes, it slowed us down a bit because I was now flying with one wing while traveling abroad. But I did not allow it to impact our trip negatively. In no way was I going to dampen this experience for my friend. While I was certain my wrist was broken, I told her that if it still hurt upon our return home, I would go to the E.R. and get it checked out.

The moment we landed at DFW International Airport on Thursday, my hand started throbbing. Excruciating pain! I've heard physicians say that bone pain is the worst physical pain there is. I believe it!

Once I arrived in town, I dropped my luggage off at home and immediately went to the emergency room where they confirmed — my wrist was broken. I was given pain meds, a temporary splint, and a referral to a specialist. A week later, I went to the orthopedic specialist who cast my hand. This was yet another painful experience because the cast has to be molded to your hand, which involves pressing upon the injured area. In order for my wrist to heal, pressure had to be applied.

After wearing the cast for several months, the day finally came for the doctor to remove it. Dead skin was sloughing off this visibly unattractive immobile hand that no longer appeared to be a part of my body. The specialist referred me to physical therapy for the next phase of healing. He stated, "Once a bone has been broken, it is changed forever. Physical therapy is required for rehabilitation."

On the second day of physical therapy, I was introduced to putty therapy, which involves marbles meshed into putty. If you've read my book, *I Got My Marbles Back*, you know I was beyond thrilled that marbles were a part of my physical therapy and healing journey of my wrist. Immediately, I knew there was about to be a powerful message conveyed to me via physical therapy.

The therapeutic exercise required pulling the marbles out of the putty with my injured hand only. Ironically, the part of my body in pain, I had to use that part!

The therapist said, "Take your time to complete the task at hand. If you want to receive full range of motion (my healing), you must complete the work."

Because of excruciating pain with every move, it took me 20 minutes to excavate those marbles from the putty. Something that would've normally taken a couple minutes took longer because of the agony involved. The pain demanded intervals of rest, so I heeded to that demand. There was residue of putty on the marbles I could not get off as my injured hand struggled against the torture.

That session made me aware of the bait of pride I had eaten. What I called ambition to operate in excellence was pride. Not wanting to appear weak as I watched my injured hand tremble uncontrollably throughout the marble excavation process.

By the end of the therapy session, I celebrated the process of pulling the marbles out of the hard place.

The therapist said, "The day will come, as you continue to do the work of healing, where the marbles will be cleaned by the hand that was once injured by a fall."

From the entire experience, I learned that healing is a process involving work. We easily accept that concept with our physical bodies. But this concept is applicable to every area of our lives where we desire to flourish. We must do the work!

If you want to be debt free, you must develop a budget and strategy for debt freedom. If you want to lose weight, you must change your lifestyle by changing your destructive habits, eat healthy and exercise. You get the point I'm making?

You may push past the pain, as I did initially with my hand, but eventually, you must face it and work through the process and phases to heal. In the same way, griefwork is an unavoidable part of the grief process.

MISCONCEPTIONS ABOUT GRIEF AND THE PANDEMIC

There is a gross misconception about grief and its impact upon our lives. American society is considered a death denying culture. This belief affects the way we respond to end-of-life topics and mortality in general. However, COVID-19, the world pandemic that shook the planet through most of 2020, forced us to deal with grief and loss by the masses. The pandemic brought grief awareness to the forefront of our lives like never before.

One misconception about grief is that it always involves death. In reality, grief is not about death only but about loss.

As I write this book, many are experiencing grief due to the pandemic, whether they recognize it or not. At the same time, more people recognize the need to talk about their grief, because the pressure of the pandemic is forcing people to deal with unaddressed issues in their lives. Many are grieving not only the countless deaths but also loss of jobs, homes, cars, physical and mental health, socialization, normalcy, etc. Pastors and ministry leaders are grieving the lack of their congregations gathering. Students grieve, missing their friends and canceled school activities. Administrators and teachers grieve former teaching methods. The pandemic of 2020 greatly impacted how we grieve by minimizing the needed socialization regarding funerals.

Another misconception is to avoid dealing with the loss. Pray, suppress your emotions, and keep it moving. This response is a train wreck waiting to happen because unresolved grief does not disappear into thin air. It lays dormant in your body, awaiting the next life crises to implode and explode. The impact and lingering effects of COVID-19 will be felt in the years to come as we all grapple with grief and creating a new normalcy.

Essential workers on the frontline are experiencing the grip of grief. The top E.R. doctor, who treated virus patients in a Manhattan hospital hit hard by the coronavirus outbreak, died by suicide. The following excerpt shares further about her journey.

> Dr. Breen's father, Dr. Philip C. Breen, said she
> had described devastating scenes of the toll the

coronavirus took on patients. "She tried to do her job, and it killed her," he said.

The elder Dr. Breen said his daughter had contracted the coronavirus but had gone back to work after recuperating for about a week and a half. The hospital sent her home again, before her family intervened to bring her to Charlottesville, he said.

Dr. Breen, 49, did not have a history of mental illness, her father said. But he said that when he last spoke with her, she seemed detached, and he could tell something was wrong. She had described to him an onslaught of patients who were dying before they could even be taken out of ambulances. [3]

The gripping reality of grief hits hard for those on the front line, but it also attacks others impacted by the virus. From Dr. Breen to a flight attendant giving an emotional and tearful farewell to the passengers and crew on her last flight. She faces an uncertain future due to being furloughed because of the pandemic's impact on the airline industry.

None of us can escape the grief caused by COVID-19, whether we experience small affects or those large enough to overwhelm the strongest person. Whether we find our world turned upside down or merely inconvenienced, we all must deal with some degree of angst during times like these.

---

[3] (Ali Watkins 2020)

GRIEFWORK

Griefwork is essential, not optional. It's imperative that everyone takes personal responsibility in doing the work of grief. Doing your griefwork is no easy task. It's the psychological process of coping with a significant loss. For many, grief is not acknowledged nor perceived as work. For others, they are simply unaware of the impact of grief and the work involved. It demands that you exert emotional and physical energy, draining you to the extent that simple tasks become difficult.

Your griefwork also entails not only your death losses but loss of any kind—such as loss of health, relationships, job, housing, dreams, hopes, your future. For example, a widower must grieve and mourn not only her husband but also for the retirement they will not share. I recall a bereaved parent whose teenage daughter died, and the mother grieved during prom time because she and her daughter didn't get the opportunity to experience prom.

Erich Lindemann is one of the pioneers in the grief industry. He coined the term griefwork after the catastrophic fire at Boston's Cocoanut Grove Night Club, the worst disaster at that time, where nearly 500 people perished. Lindemann and his colleagues undertook the first systemic study and approach to grief by interviewing the family members who lost loved ones in that tragedy.

As mentioned in the previous chapter, grief is universal yet unique. It is an internal, profound emotional response to loss which impacts our biological system. Simply put, if you don't deal with your grief, it will deal with you. Meaning, you can become physically sick as a direct result of not processing your grief, which is experienced physically, spiritually, emotionally, and behaviorally and has a way of marching into our lives and altering them forever. No one can change the reality of death and grief. However, we can change the way we respond when it occurs. Grieving is a natural healing process that slowly leads from the pain of loss to hope for the future.

The word grief is derived from the Latin meaning to burden. The weight of grief is indeed burdensome, thus the need for you to participate in some form of grief support because every loss deserves to be mourned.

What is mourning? It is the external expression of the emotions on the inside. Mourning is a learned behavior that moves you through the grief process. It is the outward expression of grief. Any action that helps you adjust and adapt to your loss is considered mourning.

Examples of mourning:
Crying
Talking about the loss
Exercising
Gardening
Journaling
Reading
and the list goes on.

When going through grief or helping others through it, it's important to understand the language of grief.

Griefwork:	process of working through grief reactions.
Bereavement:	the event of suffering the loss of a loved one.
Grief Wounds:	emotional trauma causes damage to the emotional, psychological, or spiritual component of an individual. Like physical wounds, healing occurs from the inside out.
Grief Bursts:	unexpected emotional reactions.
Grief Triggers:	music, pictures, dates, sights, smells, etc. Anything can trigger a grief moment.
Normal Grief:	one is able to progress through the pain of grief in a healthy manner.

Complicated
Grief: one exhibits behaviors resulting from intense, overwhelming grief that has extreme difficulty processing through grief in a healthy manner.

Disenfranchised Grief, coined by Dr. Ken Doka "Grief that persons experience when they incur a loss that is not or cannot be openly acknowledged, socially sanctioned or publicly mourned."

Dr. Ken Doka suggests this can happen for a number of reasons that, for the most part, fall into one (or sometimes more) of the following categories:

1. The loss isn't seen as worthy of grief (Ex.-non-death losses)
2. The relationship is stigmatized (Ex.-partner in an extramarital affair)
3. The mechanism of death is stigmatized (Ex.-suicide or overdose death)
4. The person grieving is not recognized as a griever (Ex.- co-workers or ex-partners)
5. The way someone is grieving is stigmatized. (Ex.-the absence of an outward grief response or extreme grief responses) [4]

Many have been experiencing Disenfranchised Grief due

---

[4] (Williams 2018)

to deaths in 2020 that have nothing to do with coronavirus.

Celebrity deaths and Fatal Shootings that made the national news:

1. NBA Star Kobe Bryant, his daughter Gianna, and eight others
2. Glee Star Naya Rivera
3. Representative John Lewis
4. Black Panther Star Chadwick Boseman
5. Supreme Court Justice Ruth Bader Ginsburg
6. Botham Jean
7. Atatiana Jefferson
8. Amad Aubrey
9. George Floyd
10. Breonna Taylor
11. Bill Withers
12. Jerry Jeff Walker
13. Eddie Van Halen
14. Helen Reddy
15. Mac Davis

and the list goes on.

Abandonment Grief, coined by Susan Anderson in *The Abandonment Recovery Workbook*

Abandonment Grief is a sense of separation as desertion. It creates grief that is not recognized by society. While you may receive support after the initial loss, it will soon wane due to the overused stigma *'let it go and move forward.'* The public at large will never understand the difficulties associated with abandonment grief because it involves feelings of rejection as well as grieving and mourning someone who is still alive.

According to Susan Anderson, "The ongoing craving for a relationship is the kingpin of abandonment grief, a need that is not intense for people grieving a death. When your loved one dies, you know that it does not reflect on your worthiness or desirability as a man or a woman. But when someone chooses not to be with you, the rejection creates a narcissistic injury—a stinging hurt that goes beyond grief and insults the self. The wound is painful and persistent. You question your own lovability and worthiness indefinitely." [5]

Grief and mourning don't necessarily happen simultaneously. However, I recommend that you allow yourself to grieve and mourn at the same time. In my practice, I have found that many don't allow the mourning process, the external expression of their grief. Therefore, it remains within and erupts later in life. Both grief and mourning are heavily influenced by culture, which affects our response when loss occurs. Some cultures handle grief more effectively than others while some cultures and faith communities have specific, designated mourning times. In actuality, you never get over grief, you adjust to it.

Historically, in America, the problem has been the stigma associated with the topics of grief, loss, death and dying. This caused most Americans to become uncomfortable with death. Many have tried to ignore that it happens. This stigma is

---

[5] (Anderson 2016)

widespread in our systems. In Corporate America, you are given approximately three to five bereavement days. Only three to five days to be over the loss and back at work within a week's time, at top performance level.

Bereavement Researcher Dr. Toni Miles says we, as a society, must do better for the grief stricken. "For over a decade, Dr. Toni Miles has studied the impact of bereavement. She is a physician with a PhD in public health. Her research indicates that a significant loss (parent, spouse, sibling, or child) is deadly serious, putting you, the griever, at higher risk for serious health problems, and even their own premature death." [6]

I recall a middle-aged male grief-group participant who attended my grief support group years ago. He attended the group because his wife died, and his doctor mandated he participate in some form of grief support. Per the participant, the doctor shared data that the majority of his male patients at that time were suffering from diseases such as prostate cancer, bladder cancer, ulcers, all because of unaddressed grief and emotional pain.

Queen Elizabeth said, "Grief is the price we pay for love." Why does the pain hurt so badly? It's because you loved so hard. You loved one may have died, but your love for them did not die. Thomas Lynch stated, "If we want to avoid our grief, we simply avoid each other." Grief is definitely part of what it means to be human. We were created to be in relationship with one another. We are social beings with the

[6] (Burger 2019)

need to receive and express love. So when you love and lose that love, you grieve.

I know what it feels like to avoid dealing with grief as well as to process grief due to personal loss. It comes in waves and initially feels like a tsunami is drowning you. Once you start doing your griefwork, the waves of grief subside, giving you time to breathe. I felt the excruciating pain of a divorce, the loss of my marriage. I grieved and mourned that death and the many losses that came with it.

The process of doing your *griefwork* looks different for everyone. Many have asked, "What does it mean to do your *griefwork*?" It means doing the work of healing, whatever that is for you — counseling, therapy, journaling, exercising, and the list goes on.

At some point in life, we all endure trauma that leaves grief in its wake. The cause or depth differs, but in each instance we owe it to ourselves and our overall well-being to process through the sorrow. Part of griefwork includes allowing ourselves to mourn, and we need not feel guilt or shame over our mourning. In the same way a person with a physical injury might show outward signs of pain, we have the right to show signs of our grief. In addition, we owe it to ourselves and those who love us to do the work of mourning for the amount of time we need until we experience healing. Dr. Alan D. Wolfelt penned a bill of rights, and it applies to all who mourn.

The Mourner's Bill of Rights
by Alan D. Wolfelt, Ph.D.
** denotes verbiage from the COVID-19 Bill of Rights

Though you should reach out to others as you do the work of mourning, you should not feel obligated to accept the unhelpful responses you may receive from some people. You are the one who is grieving, and as such, you have certain "rights" no one should try to take away from you. The following list is intended both to empower you to heal and to decide how others can and cannot help. This is not to discourage you from reaching out to others for help, but rather to assist you in distinguishing useful responses from hurtful ones.

**The pandemic has created unusually complicated death and grief circumstances for many people personally affected by COVID-19. If someone you love has died from the novel coronavirus, you have certain "rights" that no one can take away from you.

You have the right to experience your own unique grief.

No one else will grieve in exactly the same way you do. So when you turn to others for help, don't allow them to tell what you should or should not be feeling.

**While many people are experiencing COVID-related loss, no one else will grieve in exactly the same way you do. So, when you turn to others for help, don't allow them to tell what you should or should not be feeling.

You have the right to talk about your grief.

Talking about your grief will help you heal. Seek out others who will allow you to talk as much as you want, as often as you want, about your grief. If at times you don't feel like talking, you also have the right to be silent.

You have the right to feel a multitude of emotions.

Confusion, disorientation, fear, guilt and relief are just a few of the emotions you might feel as part of your grief journey. Find listeners who will accept your feelings without condition.

You have the right to be tolerant of your physical and emotional limits.

Your feelings of loss and sadness will probably leave you feeling fatigued. Respect what your body and mind are telling you. Get daily rest. Eat balanced meals. And don't allow others to push you into doing things you don't feel ready to do.

You have the right to experience "griefbursts."

Sometimes, out of nowhere, a powerful surge of grief may overcome you. This can be frightening but is normal and natural. Find someone who understands and will let you talk it out.

You have the right to make use of ritual.

The funeral ritual does more than acknowledge the death

of someone loved. It helps provide you with the support of caring people. More importantly, the funeral is a way for you to mourn. If others tell you the funeral or other healing rituals such as these are silly or unnecessary, don't listen.

**Death rituals such as funerals not only help you truly acknowledge a death and express your necessary feelings, but they also bring friends and family together to support one another. Funerals are especially important in circumstances in which you could not be with the dying person or view the body. If pandemic restrictions prevented a meaningful funeral shortly after the death, you have the right to have one or more gatherings in the months to come.

You have the right to embrace your spirituality.

If faith is a part of your life, express it in ways that seem appropriate to you. Allow yourself to be around people who understand and support your religious beliefs.

You have the right to search for meaning.

You may find yourself asking, "Why did he or she die? Why this way? Why now?" Some of your questions may have answers, but some may not. Watch out for the clichéd responses some people may give you. Comments like "It was God's will" or "Think of what you have to be thankful for" are not helpful, and you do not have to accept them.

You have the right to treasure your memories.

Memories are one of the best legacies that exist after the death of someone loved. You will always remember. Instead of ignoring your memories, find others with whom you can share them.

You have the right to move toward your grief and heal.

Reconciling your grief will not happen quickly. Remember, grief is a process, not an event. Be patient and tolerant with yourself. Neither you nor those around you must forget that the death of someone loved changes your life forever. 7

**Your grief has been complicated by extremely difficult circumstances, and reconciling it will not happen quickly. Be patient and gentle with yourself, and avoid people who are impatient and intolerant with you. The more you actively embrace and express your grief—bit-by-bit, day-by-day—the

---

[7] (Alan D. Wofelt 2016)

more momentum you will achieve toward healing. 8

[8] (Dr. Alan Wofelt 2020)

Pivotal Moment: an important point that signifies a shift in direction

How you handle your pivot is going to impact your outcome.

My griefwork began when I recognized I was depressed and suicidal about the separation and subsequent divorce. I went to the doctor for antidepressants in an effort to cope with the grief. My doctor wanted to admit me to the mental health hospital during our appointment. I refused because I was in denial of my status. I was experiencing complicated grief. I finally succumbed to the emotional pain and admitted myself into the mental health hospital for treatment. It was there my healing began.

Identify your pivotal moment(s) that unveiled the need to do your griefwork.

_____

_____

_____

_____

_____

_____

Recovery Toolkit: excavation and irrigation tools

Take a moment and examine your life to determine what griefwork you need to do (e.g. counseling, medication, journaling, talking with perpetrator). Identify losses you have not mourned and plan your griefwork.

_____

_____

_____

_____

_____

_____

_____

_____

_____

_____

_____

_____

Part II
Overcoming
Depression

I Got My Marbles Back
and
still depressed.
It's more than just a case of the blues.

The Grief Doctor

Chapter 4
The Dark Cloud of Depression

You know when you feel the weight of sadness,
You may feel exhausted, hopeless, and anxious
Whatever you do, you feel lonely and don't
enjoy the things you once loved.
Things just don't feel like they use to
These are some symptoms of depression, a
serious medical condition affecting over 20
million Americans.
While the cause is unknown, depression may be
related to an imbalance of natural chemicals
between nerve cells in the brain,
Prescription Zoloft works to correct this
imbalance
You shouldn't have to feel this way.
Only a doctor can diagnose depression.
*When you know more about what's wrong, you
can help make it right.* [9]

This Zoloft Commercial aired almost 20 years ago, and I

---

[9] (Pfizer Pharmaceuticals 2001)

still remember it today because it depicts the sentiments of my struggle with depression. I felt like that little ball in the commercial with a sad face and a perpetual dark cloud hovering over its head.

With the help of God and participating in my own healing (doing my griefwork), I was able to press through the depression of the divorce. Yes, I got my marbles back and experienced spurts of happiness but still exhibited signs and symptoms of depression. I was silently suffering behind closed doors in fear of judgement. Too fearful to even seek help on a consistent basis or even talk about it.

During my research on this topic, I learned that many pastors and spiritual leaders suffer from depression due to the high profile, high-stress position of Senior Pastor. I can recall many occasions I preached powerfully under the anointing of God, only to go home and ball up in the fetal position, crying over what I perceived as a failed assignment. My mind was a constant battlefield for the enemy to play tricks on me. Self-sabotaging behavior became the norm by bombarding myself with statements like, "Tonya, you forgot to say this or you should've said that," so on and so forth.

I know firsthand that God uses yielded but broken vessels. Although I was thankful to get my marbles back, it was a daily fight to keep them! This is why there is no room for judgement. We never know what others are going through privately. I know many wonder why I go hard in praise and worship. It's because that's how I fight my battles. It has kept me grounded enough to live another day.

Truthfully, the divorce wasn't the first time I felt like a

black cloud was hovering over me. I have felt this way all of my life but didn't know it was depression. Culturally, we didn't discuss issues such as this. I had grown accustomed to feeling sad, lonely, and timid, thinking it was the norm. I thought feeling sad, stuck, isolated, and lonely was a part of my destiny. I didn't have the emotional and spiritual strength to know or declare anything different.

I had become a professional mask wearer, hiding the depth of my emotional pain. Before getting married, I could mask it well until I slid down that slippery slope of depression. Then my family and friends noticed because I would isolate myself and cry until I couldn't cry any longer.

When I got married and became a First Lady, I had to up my masquerade game. I got better at masking pain until it began to unravel toward the end of the marriage. I can recall a moment when my then husband stood next to me while I sat at my desk. We had just discussed separating. I was so devastated I was staring into space.

I recall him softly uttering the words, "She gon' lose her mind."

Guess what? He was right!

I did lose my marbles, but not solely because of our marital problems. I discovered this year it happened because the depression was already present in my life. The break up was the catalyst that sent me over the edge.

Downtime during the quarantine of COVID-19 forced me to take a really good look at me. Immediately, I strolled through the corridors of my mind and envisioned the multiple times depression overshadowed me.

1. I was a timid child, feelings easily hurt
2. Suicidal on two occasions behind a relationship break up with a man
3. Almost dropped out of college because I failed a math class

GRIEF AND DEPRESSION

Depression in its mildest form is sadness experienced after a loss. Feeling depressed is a normal part of the grief process. Grief Pioneer, Dr. Elizabeth Kubler Ross, mentions depression as one of the Stages of Grief:

- Feeling depressed and hopeless after the loss of a significant other is common
- Social withdrawal and loss of interest in the outside world
- Simple tasks become difficult (getting out of bed, going to work, taking care of business, etc.)
- Crying is a normal response

However, prolonged periods of depression can lead to irrational despair causing other behavioral concerns: suicidal thoughts, alcohol or drug abuse, etc. Individuals should seek professional assistance during this time. This is clinical depression, a mental health condition that is diagnosable by a doctor. It's an imbalance of natural chemicals between nerve cells in the brain. It affects mood, thinking, and behavior. It's debilitating.

Grief and depression can be experienced simultaneously, but they are not the same. Chronic depression is an illness that is diagnosed based upon duration and intensity.

Many Christians struggle with depression, suffering silently as I did. Ecclesiastes 1:9 gives us to know that there is nothing new under the sun. Depression existed long before our time. In Psalm 42, we see that King David was no stranger to depression.

My recommendation is that some of us need prayer, counseling, and the pill. Taking prescribed medicine does not show a lack of faith in God. The medicine addresses the brain dysfunction, the chemical imbalance. Sometimes the medication is needed temporarily to help you cope until things level out. Perform your due diligence in researching the side effects of medications. If you don't feel comfortable taking prescribed medication, seek out herbal remedies to aid you through the depression.

You can also learn to conquer depression from a spiritual approach with the Word of God. Here's the challenge. When your mind is injured emotionally due to grief or trauma, it's difficult to engage in any kind of activity, especially spiritual. Surround yourself with those you trust that are well rounded and grounded in both the spiritual and natural realms to support you through it.

PANDEMIC DEPRESSION

Earlier this year, in March, I decided to contact my PCP for antidepressants because I was just not getting better. The struggle with depression had intensified. I couldn't muster up enough strength to schedule an appointment with a therapist.

I was at my wit's end.

Imagine that—The Grief Doctor, helping countless others heal but couldn't receive my healing. That alone brought frustration and anxiety to the forefront of my life. I had been battling with health issues for the last five years and couldn't take it any longer (weight gain; hormonal imbalance, constant extreme fatigue, sadness, back pain, cravings, and sleep apnea). I scheduled the appointment to visit my PCP. A week later, we were under a mandatory quarantine due to COVID-19. Needless to say, my appointment was canceled because telehealth appointments had not gone into effect at that point.

In April, I picked up a book I purchased back in June 2016, Shadow Boxing by Dr. Henry Malone. This book was a game changer for me. It helped transform my life and provide clarity on what I was experiencing and why various difficulties were confronting me. This book gave me the tools to bring inner healing which was so desperately needed.

> "Mental pain is less dramatic than physical pain, but it is more common and also more hard to bear. The frequent attempt to conceal mental pain increases the burden: it is easier to say 'My tooth is aching' than to say 'My heart is broken.'"
>
> — C. S. Lewis, *The Problem of Pain*

Anyone who has suffered from depression will tell you it is hard to manage, and you feel like others don't understand or may even judge you. Most don't understand that depression is not just about being really sad. It's an illness that must be addressed.

So I dared to open Pandora's Box and learned about genetic vulnerability based on statistical data. Those of us with depressed family members are two times more susceptible to depression than those with no family history of depression. This information forced me out of denial into reality regarding my battle with depression.

My parents are deceased, so my two older sisters are my historians. Through countless questions about our family history, I was able to determine the root of my depression.

This is why the last sentence in the Zoloft Commercial resonated with me so intently. It hit me like a jackhammer and cracked open this precious reservoir of healing. The revelation of secrets can heal. It helped me understand why my family was always so protective of me and hovered over me in ways I couldn't understand. It was because they didn't want me to fall into the trap of depression as did our family.

"When you know more about what's wrong, you can help make it right."

Now that I knew more about the root of my rotten fruit of depression, I connected the dots of what was happening in my life. I wasn't crazy for feeling the weight of depression after all. This further taught me that doing my griefwork to heal was essential and necessary for me to live! I had no other option but to confront it. I was finally ready to heal—for real.

Wherever you are in life, I encourage you to keep pushing and fighting to live a healthy emotional life. In times past, I fought depression naturally (therapy and antidepressants) and spiritually (prayer, worship, and study of the Word of God) but didn't realize that I wasn't fully dressed for battle spiritually. I didn't have all the tools (gear) needed for war. I was shadow boxing with the dark side, an enemy called depression, and I was losing. Baptized in the Holy Ghost but battling with depression. How could this be?

It's because there was a missing piece to this puzzle (my armor) called revelation. Once I received the information about my family history, the revelation came.

"When the student is ready, the teacher will appear." This is a saying with great debate over the author of it. Regardless of the author, its concept speaks to me. I was finally ready to do the work to annihilate depression!

Do your work, fight through it. It's worth it!

Pivotal Moment: an important point that signifies a shift in direction

How you handle your pivot is going to impact your outcome.

Recognize that as you do your griefwork, it takes time to shed layers of past pain to get to the core of your issue. The quarantine time was the pivotal moment that forced me to go deeper in dealing with my lifelong battle of depression.

Identify your pivotal moment(s) that awakened you to the reality of depression or unresolved issues in your life.

_____

_____

_____

_____

_____

_____

_____

_____

_____

_____

Recovery Toolkit: excavation and irrigation tools

Identify areas where you have unresolved issues: hurt, depression, anxiety, addictions, etc. Then develop a plan of action to address the issue(s).

_____

_____

_____

_____

_____

_____

_____

_____

_____

_____

_____

_____

_____

If we know where we came from, we may better know where to go. If we know who we came from, we may better understand who we are.

Unknown

Chapter 5
Check Your Roots

As a grief counselor, I get the opportunity to meet people from all walks of life and of different faith backgrounds. A thread of truth I've noted in each session is that most of them perceive counseling as an avenue of addressing life crises, when in reality, counseling is also available for celebratory moments in life.

Another interesting fact is that most confuse coaching with counseling. These modalities are different modes of the 'helping profession.' Coaching helps the client work on goals for the future, to create a new life path; whereas, counseling involves examining the past, searching for root causes of present day behavior. A quote from *Criminal Minds*, one of my favorite TV shows, explains it best, "You must sit with the past before you can walk away from it."

Remember, I've only been doing my *griefwork* since the life transition of divorce in 2012. I admit that it wasn't until this year, 2020, the year that changed our world due to a global pandemic (COVID-19), that I understood the power of searching for root causes. While I have had the honor to get in the trenches and accompany many clients through their journey, it came time for me to do the same for myself.

Take a moment and assess your life and those who surround you, those who sit in the front row of your life. Think of the exhibition of maladaptive behaviors such as abuse and addictions of any kind (alcohol, drug, sex, food, physical, or emotional) that's prevalent in your life or the lives of those close to you. Honestly, there is a reason why we do what we do and why we are the way that we are. In reality, we can inherit mentalities and mindsets such as racism, poverty, sexism, depression; finding ourselves keeping *family secrets* at the expense of our own mental health and sanity.

Through working with clients, I've discovered that the ancient colloquialism of 'what happens in our house stays in our house' rings loudly not only within the black community but other cultures as well. What we see on display within our lives and others is unaddressed, unresolved issues and pain. Always remember that unresolved grief, hurt, and trauma doesn't mysteriously disappear into thin air. It lays dormant in our inner being, waiting to appear center stage of your next life crisis.

On occasion, clients will choose not to work with me because they are not ready to commit to doing their griefwork; their root work. There was one client who referred to me as 'a poker.' Initially, I was offended by that statement but asked her to explain herself.

She said, "You poke and cause people to have to deal with stuff."

I responded, "Oh, well yeah, I am a poker indeed!" And then we chuckled about it.

In actuality, it's important for us to understand the impact of past trauma. Adverse childhood experiences shaped our lives, oftentimes stunting our growth and development. We grow into adulthood physically but not mentally or emotionally due to past trauma.

We can learn from agriculture about the correlation between our root and fruit system. Every tree has a root system that was designed to hold the tree up and to nurture it for growth. When we see behaviors or rotten fruit such as anger, fears, possessiveness, rebellion, critical spirit, physical diseases, mental illness, sexual sin, etc., know that these behaviors are stemming from a root that must be pulled up and out of your life. Eliminating the roots requires excavation and irrigation in areas of your life that you've attempted to deny or suppress.

Root Cause Analysis (RCA) is a popular and often used technique (systematic process) that helps people answer the question of *why* the problem occurred in the first place. It seeks to identify the origin of a problem (root causes) using a specific set of steps, with associated tools, to find the *primary* cause of the problem, so that you can:

- determine what, why, and how it happened and;
- figure out what to do to reduce the likelihood of it happening again [10]

(Learn more about RCA from the Washington State Department of Enterprise Services.)

---

[10] (Washington State Department of Enterprise Services n.d.)

Although RCA is a systematic approach associated with organizations, it can apply to almost any situation. For every fruit (good or bad), there is a root.

We can easily trace some issues straight to the root, even though we may have a difficult time looking at them. However, sometimes, we don't remember the trauma that planted roots capable of causing extreme issues in life. Once such trauma begins, as we take our first breath, and as we try to trace smaller roots back to the main one, we may need to revisit our beginnings.

The trauma of childbirth.

The normal process of childbirth is beautiful from the mother's perspective, but from the baby's perspective, it's a traumatic experience, whether by vaginal birth or by C-section. Think about it, transitioning from a warm, snug environment (the womb) providing nutrients to passing through a small canal to an entirely different world with lights, smells, and unfamiliar sounds, stimulating senses, forcing exponential acclimation to a new environment.

It wasn't until this year that I learned about the impact of trauma from childbirth, of how I've been fighting to live since birth. As for my story, I was born into trauma—born prematurely at seven months by C-section, weighing in at 3 lb. 8 oz. I was immediately whisked away, separated from my mother due to complications; life expectancy for both of us was bleak.

When I began my griefwork journey in 2012, God showed

me glimpses of my past, but I didn't understand the totality of its impact until 2020.

God speaks to me in dreams and visions. Upon being admitted to outpatient therapy at the Excel Center in 2012, God showed me a vision of my mother in the hospital. Back then, children were not allowed on the floor to visit patients. In the vision, an adult male secretly took me to see Mama. I was around age five or six, standing in the threshold of the doorway of Mama's hospital room at St. Joseph's Hospital in Ft. Worth, Texas. There I stood, watching my mother in a hospital bed, crying and reaching for me.

I didn't understand the vision, so I called my oldest sister, Glenda, for clarity. She confirmed that the situation did happen. Daddy took me to see Mama in the hospital.

I shared with my sister then. "We need a family meeting to discuss our family history, the good, the bad, and the ugly."

She agreed to it, but it did not come to fruition until 2020. Just a couple of months before the coronavirus hit the USA in full force, I called the family history meeting. My sisters and I decided to do it on our Daddy's birthday, February 28. We celebrated his birthday by talking about our family history. Finally, we dealt with the elephant in our room.

We had a wonderful time learning about our family heritage. My two sisters served as historians, sharing about our legacy. I gleaned so much from this time together. It brought further clarity to my life experiences. My middle sister, Mildred, shared that our mother struggled with depression due to her life experiences. She also stated that depression ran in mother's lineage. So when they witnessed me struggling with depression, they hovered over me in an effort to protect me, not thinking to expose the spirit of depression over our family. Mildred identified three major episodes of depression I encountered.

1. The break up with a guy who they later found out was abusive to me.
2. During my college years, I was depressed over school and wanted to quit. My family bought me a plane ticket and told me to come home. I'll never forget, my entire family picked me up at the airport in Glenda's Goodtime Van. Again, in an effort to protect me, they didn't force me to return to school in Austin.
3. The divorce in 2012.

What my family didn't know until this meeting is that I privately struggled with many other bouts of depression.

Mildred also stated, "You are the curse breaker, the chain breaker for our family. You broke the back of depression off of you and our bloodline and we are thankful!"

Having had this long awaited family discussion, healing began to spring forth in my life exponentially! The pieces of my puzzles were finally coming together, the good and the bad, creating the beautiful tapestry of my life. I gained a greater understanding of my thought life, my lifelong struggle with depression. This family discussion helped each of us understand our behaviors and responses to life.

Here's a little bit of the revelation received from that family time of sharing, *spilling the beans*.

- Our life experiences shaped our parenting skills.

- My sisters' childhood experiences were totally different from mine because of our age gap.

- Strength was gained as we dared to confront our family secrets.

- Some of the struggles I encountered in life were not mine to carry. They came from my lineage: depression, timidity, abandonment, and rejection. It's possible to trace characteristics through families (depression, bitterness, pride and arrogance, manipulation, prejudice, violence, physical infirmities, insanity, divorce, alcoholism, suicides, criminal behavior, etc.). [11]

- I identified the root causes, familial spirits: depression, rejection, and abandonment.

- Although I began my *griefwork* in 2012, I learned that I was healed in certain areas, but not whole. This family conversation brought wholeness to my life.

Exposing our family secrets brought healing to each of us that were open to it. Through the power of God, I gracefully and successfully fought and conquered depression and all the familial spirits attached to it!

You don't like what you see in your family? You have the power to change your family tree by doing the work to heal

---

[11] (Malone 1999)

and experience a healthy life. It's important to address your family relational issues because they influence how we move through life.

Check your root system and cultivate it!

Pivotal Moment: an important point that signifies a shift in direction

How you handle your pivot is going to impact your outcome.

The pivotal moment was when I mustered up the nerve to request a family meeting to discuss our history, issues, etc.

Identify a moment when you recognized unhealthy commonalities in your family lineage and the need for change.

_____

_____

_____

_____

_____

_____

_____

_____

_____

_____

_____

Recovery Toolkit: excavation and irrigation tools

Assess and determine if you are willing to participate and possibly facilitate a family meeting. Please be aware that all family members are not in the same space as you and may not participate. Identify those unhealthy commonalities in your family and be willing to determine a plan of action to address family issues that impact you. Journal your thoughts concerning this.

_____

_____

_____

_____

_____

_____

_____

_____

_____

_____

_____

Check Your Roots

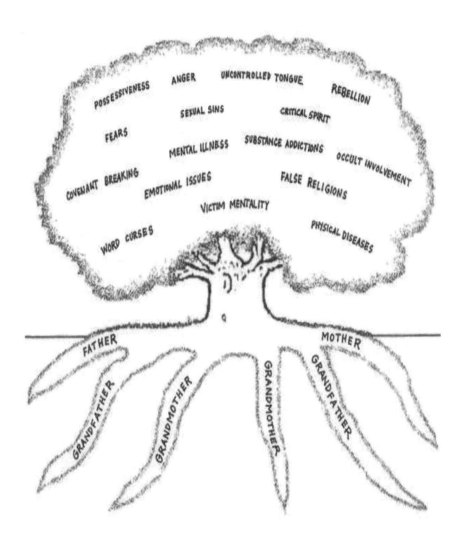

Part III
Overcoming
Rejection

A clear
REJECTION
is better than a
FAKE
promise.

Unknown

Chapter 6
The Danger of Rejection

"Every time I thought I was being rejected from something good, I was actually being redirected to something better."
Dr. Steve Maraboli

Google definition of *reject*:
Verb - dismiss as inadequate, inappropriate, or not to one's taste.
Noun - a person or thing dismissed as failing to meet standards or satisfy tastes.

Rejection is a part of life, and every human being experiences it, from the womb to the elderly. None of us are exempt. We experience it on a regular basis on many levels such as:

- The impact of an unwanted pregnancy on a baby

- The little kid who wasn't picked to play on the neighborhood basketball team

- The student who didn't receive the scholarship

- The adult who didn't get the job or promotion

- Abandoned by a spouse or parent

- Social rejection of the elderly in a retirement or nursing home

- The inability to show love and affection through verbal expression of "I love you" or provision of basic needs such as food, shelter, and clothing

- Being widowed

- Infidelity

- Betrayal

The danger of rejection is that it begins early in life, and we are not taught how to handle it in a healthy way. This starts us off on an unsteady course in life, making it difficult to handle any other rejection. That is what happened to me.

When my husband decided to leave the marriage covenant, I felt the highest level of rejection and betrayal. Questions, like marbles, began to roll around in my head. What do you do when the one you love no longer loves you? How do you handle life when your faith and feelings collide? When I discovered that what I invested my identity in no longer was attached to me, I fell into the pit of despair. Not realizing all along that the seed of rejection had already been planted and taken root in my life. It began in the womb.

Through research, I discovered the impact of rejection from the womb. Prenatal rejection occurs when:

- The pregnancy is unwanted

- There is infidelity present through an extra-marital affair

- The mother was molested or raped

- The parents desire a specific gender but the now popular gender reveal shows that the baby is the opposite sex

- Mother and baby bonding doesn't happen immediately after birth

- Born by C-section can cause some children to develop a spirit of rejection

As a result of these life experiences, rejection frays the fabric of your life, affecting the way you view relationships, leaving you with poor relational intelligence.

My story

Due to health complications my mother experienced at childbirth, I was born prematurely by C-section and did not get the opportunity to bond with my mother or any other family member until days later. One of the other jewels discovered during our family discussion time mentioned in the previous chapter is that my oldest sister was the first to hold me, thus the mother-daughter bond was initiated with her and not our birth mother.

While I love my birth mother, and we had the best relationship possible with the tools we had at that time, there was always this unspoken disconnect. It left me searching for approval and attention throughout my life, not realizing that my tendencies of people pleasing, perfectionism, pride, and isolation all stemmed from the root of rejection. I was born into an environment that I had to figure out how to live.

On February 24, 2020 at 8:12 a.m., just days before our monumental family meeting to discuss our family secrets and before the world was quarantined due to the coronavirus, a friend dropped an atomic bomb on me. On this significant day, the eighth-year anniversary of my former husband announcing he no longer had the capacity to be married to me any longer, my friend told me words I didn't want to hear.

She said, "Walk in your truth that your husband abandoned you for his preferred lifestyle. He's never going to apologize."

At that moment, I began to weep, not realizing that eight years post-divorce, I was still awaiting an apology from my former husband. When you are rejected by someone who identifies as being gay or bisexual, your emotional state is fragile because of the pain that kind of deceit causes.

My friend forced me out of denial I didn't know I was in. I was awaiting concrete evidence when the writing was on the wall:

- Associations (friends and acquaintances)
- Long extended absences and trips
- Mood swings
- Members of LGBTQ Community informing me of his presence

I was still protecting a unit (marriage) that broke me. That pain cut deep! It hurt worse than people will ever realize.

Many have asked, "Why did you stay in an unhealthy relationship?"

I've since learned that it was because of a term called trauma bonding which is loyalty to an unhealthy relationship. Trauma bonding occurs when emotional and traumatic experiences become the bond within a relationship, thus creating codependency. Sharie Stines, Psy.D states in her article, "What is Trauma Bonding?" that "dysfunctional marriages also cause trauma bonds because there is always a time when things seem to be 'normal.' Other types of relationships involving trauma bonds include cult-like religious organizations, kidnapping and hostage situations, those involving child abuse or incest, and unhealthy work environments. The environment necessary to create a trauma bond involves intensity, complexity, inconsistency, and a promise. Victims stay because they are holding on to that elusive promise or hope. There is always manipulation involved. So often, those in a traumatic relationship are 'looking right at it, but can't see it.' Only after time away from the unhealthy attachment can a person begin to see the destruction it caused." [12] One major sign of trauma bonding is low self-esteem. When you lose who you are in a relationship, it breeds trauma bonding, which makes it almost impossible to leave the unhealthy relationship. I lost Tonya and became First Lady.

In essence, we became trauma buddies rather than

---

[12] (Sharie Stines 2015)

husband and wife. An unhealthy relationship disguised under the cloak of religion, not realizing that trauma was the thread holding the relationship together. Over our nine year marriage, we did a lot of trauma bonding. Projecting trauma on to each other, neither one of us knew what a healthy relationship looked like for us.

After the divorce, I was living in a fog, wondering daily if I'd make it through this trial, because rejection can be a sword that pierces your soul (the seat of your emotions).

Through the help of God, a trauma team, and doing the work of healing, I've been able to push through rejection to victory! Yes, trauma requires a specialist who can aid in your healing. When healing from trauma, find your trauma team. These are individuals who can handle your trauma. This team should include a therapist trained in trauma and its impact as well as individuals who can objectively handle the weight of what's happened to you. Truthfully, your pastor should not nor can be your therapist. Their assignment is spiritual, which is necessary, but you also need the clinical component to heal holistically.

I discovered that brokenness is the place of rebirth! My healing journey has been in two stages: pruning and perfecting. During the journey, God has spoken prophetically over my life, placing the mantle of deliverance upon me that will bring restoration and deliverance to the mind, body, and soul. Not only for myself but also to those who have been in depression and carrying pain and grief for years.

God reestablished my priorities and relationships as well as realigned my boundaries with His, showing me how to minister to a community of people in the LGBTQ Community who sought me out for help. God taught me to minister and embrace that very thing which broke me. Half of my clientele is a part of the LGBTQ community, struggling with identity crisis, longing for peace in their life. Others simply need love and a compassionate ear to hear their heart's plea.

Through rejection, I've learned more about me — what I'm made of and what unrealistic expectations I had. I gleaned wisdom from it, which has empowered me in my comeback. I changed my perspective and discerned that my husband's rejection was not necessarily God wanting him out of my life but me realizing that he (my husband at the time) was not necessary for my future. Although it was a hard pill to swallow, I had to be okay with seeing myself as Leah in the Bible, who never won the love of her husband even though she loved him.

On May 6, 2020, I was watching Chicago Med on television. As you can see, I love drama television shows. On this particular episode, there was an interesting storyline that resonated with me. A transgender man, living as a woman, was in the emergency room. Unbeknownst to the patient, the ex-wife was accidentally called as next of kin. She didn't know about his sex change. The ex-wife arrived at the hospital. Needless to say, they were both shocked, but the ex-wife accepted the choices her ex-husband made concerning his life. They reconciled.

The ex-wife said to the nurse, "I knew something was off. I kept wondering why he shut me out. I wanted him to trust me with it. Sometimes when we hide who we are, we fear *rejection."* 13

Her words resonated with me because I uttered the same exact words. "I knew that something was off in our marriage, I just didn't know what." Because we were friends before getting married, it saddened me that my former husband didn't trust me with his truth, his concerns and struggles.

When you heal, you view things differently. Truth is, neither one of us trusted the other. I didn't trust him to love me the way I needed, and he didn't trust me to love him the way he needed. In reality, trust looks different for men than women. I've been told by men that trust for them lies within their emotions which are kept in a box under lock and key. Occasionally, they will open the box to test the waters. If for any reason, they do not sense trust, the box is closed shut. Sad part is, they say a man can be married and never open that box of trust. Needless to say, I didn't have the key to his box, but I'm okay with that reality now.

---

13 (Waxman 2019)

Pivotal Moment: an important point that signifies a shift in direction

How you handle your pivot is going to impact your outcome.

My pivotal moment that shifted me out of denial was in February 2020, when my friend shared those life-changing words with me.

Identify a moment when you recognized rejection in your life and journal about it.

_____

_____

_____

_____

_____

_____

_____

_____

_____

_____

_____

Recovery Toolkit: excavation and irrigation tools

What will you do differently to address rejection in your life?
Journal your thoughts concerning this.

_____

_____

_____

_____

_____

_____

_____

_____

_____

_____

Forgiveness does not change the past, but it does enlarge the future.

Paul Boese

Chapter 7
Forgiveness is Necessary to Heal

The importance of forgiveness cannot be underestimated. It is a process that requires our commitment to maintain an ongoing act of forgiveness on a daily basis.

I admit that this was indeed a challenge for me. In the beginning of my healing journey, I was angry and became bitter with anyone who was in the slightest degree connected to my former husband, including family, friends, and foe. In *my* head, there was this imaginary bold black line of demarcation that separated my folk from his folk. If there was an inkling that someone was team, former husband, I immediately evicted them from my orbit into outer space, cutting off all contact. It was like they were dead to me.

I didn't realize the damage I was incurring upon myself, because unforgiveness makes it impossible to heal. Unforgiveness means the refusal to release a debt owed by another person. Sadly, in my heart, I had set up a tombstone marking the day I was offended by my former husband, others, and even God. I ate the bait of Satan, which kept me bound in an unrelenting cycle of hurt and pain. Offense became my pillow of comfort at night and my solace during the day.

Unbeknownst to me, I was held in that strong grip of unforgiveness up until the beginning of 2020, when my friend caused me to realize I was awaiting an apology from my former husband.

As mentioned earlier in the book, healing is a process requiring layers of pain being peeled off your life to reach the inner core of your soul where the emotional wound resides. In his book, *Let It Go*, Bishop T.D. Jakes referenced counseling a man who struggled with pornography that led to an affair.

Here's an excerpt of his conversation, Excavating the Truth: "He didn't seem to realize that protecting her feelings led him to breaking her heart. Knowing that many women divorce never knowing what really caused the breach between them because it is so hard to get men to talk, I encouraged him to be open and honest with her regardless of the outcome." [14]

That was my plight. I was broken by a breach that I had to figure out myself through healing and partnering with God.

My former husband and I went to counseling a few times, but it didn't work because he didn't give himself to the process. I later learned he expressed to others that he never fully gave over to the counseling process because he didn't want to be married anymore. Both parties must be committed to the process of healing; otherwise, counseling is ineffective. Neither of us understood what love is; therefore, we were two

---

[14] (Jakes, 2013)

broken people trying to pick up the pieces of a broken marriage without addressing our individual brokenness. A house divided cannot stand.

Although that knowledge stung deep, other people added to the offenses — some intentionally, others never realizing they wounded me. People I considered friends abandoned me and stuck with him, adding to the betrayal. Others made comments, but meaning well, they did not understand the situation. Some tried to offer comfort, but the words they spoke hurt more than helped. Over time, multiple offenses left me raw, and eventually I had to forgive them — all of them.

While I had forgiven some of the people who offended me, I had not *totally* forgiven because I thought forgiving them and him would exonerate them from guilt. In reality, it doesn't. Instead, unforgiveness keeps you, the offended one, tied to the past forever. An apology from those who wronged you is not the only thing that will bring healing. But that is good, because most of the time, an apology never comes.

It's your choice to release the offense, and that will bring the ultimate healing. Too often, there are those who remain angry with people who are deceased or no longer in their life. And when they hold tight to the wounds rather than releasing them, those people experience a life without healing.

I encourage you to take your power back by forgiving those who may have hurt you, even if you are the offender. Relationships cannot work until we take inventory of our portion of the problem. This truth became real to me during worship at church one Sunday morning. We were partaking in Holy Communion, the minister quoting the scripture 1 Corinthians 11:23-26 (KJV):

"For I have received of the Lord that which also I delivered unto you, That the Lord Jesus the same night in which he was betrayed took bread: And when he had given thanks, he brake it, and said, 'Take, eat: this is my body, which is broken for you: this do in remembrance of me.' After the same manner also he took the cup, when he had supped, saying, 'This cup is the new testament in my blood: this do ye, as oft as ye drink it, in remembrance of me. For as often as ye eat this bread, and drink this cup, ye do shew the Lord's death till he come.'"

As he quoted the scripture, it sounded as if he was speaking directly to me with a mega horn, saying, "On the night Jesus was betrayed." It was at that defining moment forgiveness began to take root in my heart. Instantly, I became overwhelmed with unspeakable comfort, thinking, *Jesus was betrayed too, just like me!*

I had heard that scripture and read it countless times, but on this particular day, it hit home with me. The love of Christ washed over me because of His forgiveness of my sins. As human beings, especially people of faith in the Body of Christ, we have a tendency to forget God's example of forgiveness and reconciliation with us directly through His son Jesus Christ. He daily forgives me for the error of my ways. How can I not forgive those who hurt me?

It's because we don't fully understand the concept of

forgiveness. We try to forgive with our mind or our will when that is impossible to do. Forgiveness is a product of our soul and spirit, which means it's a supernatural ability given to us by God. We are triune beings made in the image of the Godhead:

- Spirit – our spirit connects with Holy Spirit, intuition, conscience
- Soul – seat of emotions, mind, and will
- Body – flesh, skin, appetite

While forgiveness begins in the mind by making the conscious decision to forgive, it goes much deeper to the inward parts of who we are, thus keeping many of us bound in torment. We must be healed of emotional trauma within our soulish realm (emotions) in order to partner with the Holy Spirit and forgive out of our spirit man (inner being).

> "Then came Peter to him, and said, 'Lord, how oft shall my brother sin against me, and I forgive him? till seven times?' Jesus saith unto him, 'I say not unto thee, Until seven times: but, Until seventy times seven.'" (Matthew 18:21-22 KJV)

Forgiveness is not an option, it's a demonstration of the life of a Christian.

> "So likewise shall my heavenly Father do also unto you, if ye from your hearts forgive not every one his brother their trespasses." (Matthew 18:35 KJV)

Here, Jesus teaches that it is from the heart that a man must forgive. The heart is the spirit or inner man. It is in our spirit that we must forgive those who hurt us, not our emotions.

Work through the pain so that you can forgive others and forgive yourself, because it's necessary to heal. Refusing to forgive not only hardens your heart, but also makes you susceptible to physical sickness and disease. Admit and repent of unforgiveness and then close the door to it.

By no means at all am I saying that forgiveness is easy. Most times it is not! How do you forgive the perpetrator who violated you or your loved one? How do you forgive murder, abuse, rape, molestation, infidelity, betrayal, rejection, deceit, abandonment, and the list goes on? You do it by participating in your own rescue — do the work to heal and partner with the Holy Spirit to forgive.

Part of forgiving my former husband involved me texting an apology to him for my part in the demise of the marriage, for holding him hostage in my heart, etc. I specifically remember texting an apology twice, once in June 2012, shortly after our separation and the other in November 2019 after I received a public prophetic word that I needed to forgive him and forgive me. I also had to forgive the institution of church which hurt me. To this day, many that were members of our local church are struggling with church hurt, refusing to connect with another local body of believers because of a public, horrible, divorce.

Lastly, know that although you forgive, some relationships will never be restored to what it was before.

Trauma changes the dynamics of who we are as human beings. Total forgiveness is not necessarily reconciliation.

However, there are some relationships that will be restored to an even greater strength as a result of forgiveness. I'm a witness to this. Just a few weeks before the release of this body of work, this book, I had lunch with the mother of the young teenage boy my husband and I took in. Through doing the work of healing and prayer, I reached out to her several times during the healing journey, but because of the hurt and trauma she and her son were experiencing, forgiveness and reconciliation couldn't take place until now. She, like me, had to work to get to the place of forgiving. We met, we hugged, we smiled, we laughed, we cried, we reconnected, we reminisced, and loved on each other. Both of us discovered that we held the missing pieces to each other's healing journeys.

Harness the power of forgiveness and make space for it. Come out from under the cloak of unforgiveness so that you can gain your mental clarity and emotional stability.

Pivotal Moment: an important point that signifies a shift in direction

How you handle your pivot is going to impact your outcome.

My pivotal moment that opened my eyes to the need to forgive fully was in November 2019 when I received the public prophetic word declaring total forgiveness must take place.

Identify a moment when you recognized the need to forgive and journal about it. Who do you need to forgive today?

_____

_____

_____

_____

_____

_____

_____

_____

_____

_____

Recovery Toolkit: excavation and irrigation tools

What steps will you take to forgive? Journal your thoughts concerning this.

_____

_____

_____

_____

_____

_____

_____

_____

_____

_____

_____

_____

An Exercise in Forgiveness

1. Make a list of who you need to forgive and the offense.
2. For each name on your list, write out a declaration (on an index card or piece of paper) that reads, "Today, I am determined to forgive (insert name of offender). I forgive you for

_____

3. Pray this prayer: Father God, I repent for allowing a painful traumatic event or circumstance to become a tombstone in my soul. I forgive anyone who wounded me and caused one of these tombs to be erected in my inner man. I apply the blood of Jesus to every area of my soul where I have set up these memorials and markers. I tear them down by the power of the cross and through the resurrection and dunamis* power. Jesus came out of the tomb through resurrection power. I release resurrection power into my tomb so that the stone of unforgiveness can be rolled away and I can be free! Amen!

~Dr. Henry Malone Deliverance Training Manual

*Dunamis = "ability to perform" (L-N); for the believer, power to achieve by applying the Lord's inherent abilities. [15]

_____

[15] (Helps Ministries Inc., 1987, 2011)

Part IV
Inner Healing and Deliverance

INNER
HEALING
is required of me,
if I intend to be
free from pain,
sorrow, and hurt
that envelops me.

Eleesha.com

Chapter 8
Let the Healing Continue

An unknown author stated, "We repeat what we don't repair."

This colloquialism is true in every sense of the word. My hope is that you are encouraged to invest in your well-being by committing to do the necessary work to heal mind, body, and soul, allowing healing to continue. Why? Because healing is a process, not a destination, a one-stop shop.

Each time we encounter emotional trauma or brokenness within our lives, inner healing needs to take place. Be aware that when you handle broken people (including yourself), you will get cut and bleed—requiring needed attention to the wounded area. Put pressure on it and stop the internal hemorrhaging so you won't bleed out from unaddressed trauma. This is what the pandemic has done, put external pressure on things we were struggling with prior to the pandemic.

My mission is to provoke you to change, to cause you to shift from surviving to thriving and start living versus just existing. Shave off calloused hurt from the past so you can live again! Peel back the layers of hurt and determine what to do and what not to do. Walk through the pain to heal. If this middle-aged woman can do it, so can you!

This is the hard part because most people don't want to experience pain. Be willing to let the healing continue as new developments unfold in your life. Break destructive cycles because they erode over time. Give up the right to be right. You won't ever win that battle. I tried, it doesn't work.

You'll discover that old habits and patterns will cease as you replace them with inner healing because transformation begins within, in the deepest parts of your soul.

It wasn't until we were in the pandemic that I realized the need to go deeper in healing after continuing to battle with depression. Counseling is great, and I highly recommend it. However, some of us, and I dare say most of us, need inner healing, which goes deeper than counseling. This involves the spiritual component of inner healing and deliverance, taking back legal ground given over to forces of evil. Whether we believe it or not, there is an unseen spiritual realm out there where evil opposes good. This is the reason for the turmoil seen in our nation and world today—lots of evil, spiritual activity going on, causing people to fall into the pit of despair.

Self-care (mind, body, and soul) is vital because these portals or doorways allow entrance into our lives. As you go deeper in healing, you'll discover that some of what you struggle with (depression, anxiety, pornography, alcoholism, addictions, etc.) is not from you but from ancient doors opened in your bloodline, your family. Unforgiveness and Emotional Trauma are popular doorways to your soul, wreaking havoc in your life when unaddressed. You *can* get to the place where you are no longer offended by that which wounded you, but you must first deal with the aftermath of stacked trauma. Spend time doing your *griefwork*, excavating, irrigating, and cultivating the soil of your soul. Some clinicians refer to it as *soul work* and *heart work*.

I spent the time granted during the pandemic to do some inner healing and training. Because we were quarantined, my appointment with my PCP had to be canceled. I couldn't get the antidepressants I thought I so desperately needed at that time. I got in the trenches, just me and God, and did the hard work of healing: asking my family historians hard questions about our lineage, praying without ceasing, reading and learning about inner healing and deliverance. I went through several personal deliverance sessions with a trained Inner Healing and Deliverance Minister. She helped break the back of depression, grief, abandonment and many other things off my life! This enabled me to walk in a greater freedom in God, empowered and anointed to pull others out of depression, grief, rejection, etc., to stand in my truth and declare my healing.

In this eighth year post divorce, I can finally breathe and embrace my new beginning.

As I wrap up this book, let me encourage you in your *griefwork*. Make the commitment. Moments will arise when you feel like you can't continue, when you can't walk in that place that needs healing most. Make a decision now that you won't stop. Continue with the work in every broken area of your life.

Remember, healing is a process with many layers. And

peeling those layers takes time. While some wounds happen fast, the damage builds over time. Additional pain grows over the years when new hurts hit that old wound. Keep in mind, you didn't get this way overnight, neither will you heal from it in one moment.

As believers, we pray for healing and expect a miracle. Yes, God can do that, and He may choose to do so in your life. More than likely, healing won't be an immediate miracle. Remember my broken wrist? God didn't heal that miraculously without pain. It took months in a cast and more time with physical therapy. The healing of emotional and spiritual trauma takes time as well.

Above all, admit your brokenness. Find that safe place where you can express honestly about the depth of your shattered soul. Take courage and embrace authentic conversations with your spouse, significant other, children, siblings, parents, etc. Do not fear their answers, for they likely have broken places too. But together with them and the Holy Spirit, you can find healing — the kind of healing that is total and real, capable of lasting through this life and forever.

Works Cited

Alan D. Wofelt, P. (2016, November 22). *The Mourner's Bill of Rights.* Retrieved October 2020, from Center for Loss & Life Transition: https://www.centerforloss.com/2016/11/mourners-bill-rights/#:~:text=%20The%20Mourner%E2%80%99s%20Bill%20of%20Rights%20%201,emotions%0AConfusion%2C%20disorientat ion%2C%20fear%2C%20guilt%20and%20relief...%20More

Ali Watkins, M. R. (2020, April 27, 29). Top E.R. Doctor Who Treated Virus Patients Dies by Suicide. *The New York Times.*

Anderson, S. (2016). *The Abandonment Recovery Workbook.* Novato, CA, USA: New World Library; Workbook edition.

Burger, K. (2019, February 19). *Bereavement Researcher: We Must Do Better for the Grief-Stricken.* Retrieved October 31, 2020, from nextavenue.org: https://www.nextavenue.org/bereavement-researcher-grief-stricken/

Cunningham, T. (2015). *I Got My Marbles Back: There IS Life After Loss.* Fort Worth: Tonya Cunningham Ministries.

Dean, L. (2019). *My Creative Life: Rediscover Your Creativity.* New York: CICO of Ryland Peters & Small Ltd.

Dr. Alan Wofelt, C. f. (2020). *The COVID-19 Mourner's Bill of Rights.* Retrieved October 31, 2020, from batesville.com: https://www.batesville.com/drwolfelt-mourners-bill/

Helps Ministries Inc. (1987, 2011). *1411:Dunamis.* Retrieved November 1, 2020, from Biblehub.com: https://biblehub.com/greek/1411.htm

Jakes, T. (2013). *Let it Go: Forgive So You Can Be Forgiven.* New York, NY, USA: Atria a Division of Simon & Schuster, Inc.

Malone, H. (1999). *Shadow Boxing.* Lewisville: Vision Life Ministries International Inc.

Pfizer Pharmaceuticals. (2001). Original Zoloft Commercial. *YouTube upload 2009*. Pfizer Pharmaceuticals.

Sharie Stines, P. D. (2015, October 23). *What is Trauma Bonding?* Retrieved October 2020, from Psych Central Professional: https://pro.psychcentral.com/recovery-expert/2015/10/what-is-trauma-bonding/

Washington State Department of Enterprise Services . (n.d.). *Root Cause Analysis*. Retrieved October 2020, from https://des.wa.gov/services/risk-management/about-risk-management/enterprise-risk-management/root-cause-analysis#:~:text=Root%20cause%20analysis%20(RCA)%20is,a%20way%20to%20prevent%20them

Waxman, M. (Director). (2019). *Chicago Med* [Motion Picture].

Williams, L. (2018, April 2). *64 Examples of Disenfranchised Grief.* Retrieved October 31, 2020, from What's Your Grief: https://whatsyourgrief.com/64-examples-of-disenfranchised-grief/

About the Author

Dr. Tonya Cunningham is a Speaker, Grief Counselor, Transitional Life Coach, and Author with emphasis on loss and life transitions. She possesses a heart for people who are experiencing grief and trauma of any kind. Her unique yet transparent approach empowers others to navigate through their maze of hurt to a peaceful place of healing. She is blazing a trail to healing with a captivating message that offers practical and relevant tools that speak to the intellect and the heart of others. She encourages and empowers people to take a leap and build a 'new' life after a traumatic event has destroyed the life they once knew. Perhaps best known for her mantra, "There IS life after loss, it's just a different one," Tonya is committed to educating others on the importance of doing their griefwork, taking care of their mental health.

An advocate of higher learning, Tonya holds five degrees, including a Doctorate of Religious Philosophy in Pastoral Psychology as well as Certificates of Completion in several specialty areas: Suicide Prevention, Grief, Trauma, & Crisis Counseling, Marriage Therapy, and Chaplaincy. With over 30 years of professional experience in the grief and death care industry as a Mortician, Hospice Social Worker, Bereavement Coordinator, and Mortuary College Instructor, Tonya now provides training and personal development services such as counseling, coaching, seminars, and workshops.

Tonya is actively involved in the community by providing support services through collaboration with several funeral homes throughout the Texas region. Tonya travels extensively, speaking in corporate America and faith-based settings concerning grief, loss and life transitions, teaching others to do their griefwork which fosters healing. She is the renowned author of the book, *I Got My Marbles Back*, in which she unapologetically shares her incredible story of surviving domestic violence, death loss, divorce, and depression to promote healing. Because of the powerful impact the book has made on hundreds of people, she is now known as "The Marble Lady and The Grief Doctor."

Tonya is the mother of Chelsea, who resides in heaven, adopted son, D'Anthony and the proud Dog Mom of Mister Cunningham, her Westie.

Learn more at www.drtonyacunningham.com

BOOK DR. TONYA TO SPEAK AT YOUR NEXT EVENT

If you're looking for a speaker for your next event, Dr. Tonya Cunningham is happy to share her expertise, experience, and wisdom with your group. She's available to speak on a variety of topics, covering Grief & Loss, Inner Healing, Relationships, and Leadership.

- Conferences
- Workshops
- Retreats
- Seminars
- Trainings

She serves as a national resource on Grief & Loss, traveling across the nation to educate others on the importance of doing their griefwork and taking care of their mental health. Speaking from the core of her own experiences and education, Dr. Tonya developed the unique multi-faceted, God-given ability to connect with people of all cultures and generations, both professionally and spiritually. Sharing her captivating message of hope and healing is sure to speak to the heart of your audience.

Dr. Tonya is a promoter of healing and desires that all will commit to the process of inner healing. She takes great pride in her work, which requires extensive preparation, time, and energy.

Examples of Speaking Topics Include:

- I Got My Marbles Back!
- From Loss to Life
- I'm a Leader and I'm Depressed
- Get Your House In Order
- Not Just Another Dead-End Job
- The Empty Chair During the Holidays Grief Symposium
- How to Keep It Together When You Feel Like Falling Apart—Caring for the Caregiver
- The Elephant in the Room… Let's Deal With It

Submit booking request via website

www.drtonyacunningham.com

Other Books/Programs by Dr. Tonya

I Got My Marbles Back: There IS Life After Loss

From Loss to Life Self-Study Program: A Practical Guide on Navigating Pain to Experience Inner Healing

Visit website for details
www.drtonyacunningham.com
Transforming Lives, One at a Time

Made in the USA
Columbia, SC
12 February 2023

11930793R00070